MW00805917

WINNING
THINKING

HOW TO BE HAPPY ALMOST ALL OF THE TIME

BY

DR. MICHAEL CORTSON

Mike Cortson Company
ALL RIGHTS RESERVED

COPYRIGHT © 2006

Michael Cortson

"Attention: Permissions Coordinator, "at the address below:
The Mike Cortson Company

9587 Red Arrow Hwy. Suite 305
Bridgman, MI 49106
(269) 326-0736

Individual sales: This book is available through most bookstores or can be ordered directly from Mike Cortson Company at the address above.
Quantity sales: Special discounts are available on quantity purchases by corporations, associations and others. For details, contact the "Special Sales Department" at the publisher's address above.
Printed in the United States of America
Library of Congress Cataloging-in-Publication Data is available from the publisher.

ISBN – 0-9767346-1-3 ISBN 13 - 978-0-9767346-1-1

Foreword

President William Henry Harrison said, "I contend that the strongest of all governments is that which is most free." Mike Cortson has taken our nations strength and built an understanding of the human condition on that freedom. His new book has the courage to take a stand for the Winning Ways that we can all possess. I encourage you to read it and tell others about this adventure.

--

Dr. Ludwig Otto
www.franklinpublishing.net

Michael Cortson

WHAT ARE YOU THINKING?

Over the centuries one thing seems to be unanimous if you look at the writings of the great scholars, "these are trying times." Man throughout time has always had that in common, trying times. Even when we look back at times that we refer to as "the good old days" the people living through that period would tell you "these are trying times." I doubt there would be much disagreement with this harmless premise. Today, as always, "these are trying times."

With that said; how do people cope with these times and better still how do they improve upon them? One first has to understand the nature of man's existence right from the start. I have found there are two components to man's existence; 1) being alive, and 2) living. One would argue that these components are one in the same. I offer for semantics sake the argument that there has to be a distinction made between the two and I should define the principles. "Being alive" is the

2

physical, biological components of the body functions. Deep set in the inner core of the brain we find man's involuntary functions, i.e. breathing, heartbeat, gag reflex etc. "Living" is man's awareness and interaction with the world around him which of course is sustained via being alive. So the distinction should not be ignored. Living is thought. Thought is the chemical reactions within the structure of the brain that is ever changing and subject to all sorts of impressions voluntary and involuntary.

It is a well settled premise that man thinks in pictures accompanied by sound and then closely followed by touch and smell. Everything one has been exposed to from birth is stored in the brain just like so many records in a jukebox. By way of illustration if I asked you, "Who was your favorite teacher?" you would immediately start gathering up all of the teacher memories you have in

3

mind and instantly make a choice as to which one was your favorite. Once you made that choice you would then start recalling or "seeing" that person's face again, the classroom, and then the sound of the person's voice until the picture was complete. Now what I just did was "push your buttons". We all are familiar with the phrase. I pressed your "favorite teacher" button and you played the record. That is how your brain works.

Each day our buttons are pushed all day long. And we push quite a few ourselves. That is not to say that pushing buttons is always a negative thing to do. Certainly if a golf ball was flying out of control at some innocent person you would quickly press your own "fore" button then scream the word out thereby pressing the other person's "fore" button in hopes of having that person get out of harm's way. A closer analysis of this scenario reveals that when we pressed our own "fore"

4

button that was a choice. CHOICE is the key to advanced critical thinking. Once we were confronted with this trying situation of an errant golf shot that stimulus pressed the button in us to yell "fore". We had been taught at some point in our lives that if we hit a golf shot that could hit someone else it was proper to yell "fore" and we "instinctively" yelled the word. I submit that this was not "instinct" but more properly defined as a finely tuned choice made so quickly, since time is of the essence under those circumstances, we "programmed" ourselves to "react" as fast as if we were trying to buzz in with the correct question on television's "Jeopardy".

Man prizes his ability to choose his thoughts to a point where they are almost automatic. "Almost" is the key here. We all tend to revere those who can muster up the correct answer to a complex question the fastest.

5

Another example is preparing for a spelling bee. We try to cram as many correctly spelled words in our head as possible. In a spelling bee time is generally not an issue. Of course commonly spelled words come to each of us faster than obscure ones. The process we go through in recording these words in preparation for the spelling bee is exactly the same process we use for everything we learn. We learn to cook, read, spell, being happy, angry, sad etc... all the same way. I deliberately included emotions. Just as we choose to record the words in our mind for instant recall when we hear the word presented to us at the spelling bee, so too do we do the same thing with our emotions. Emotions are prize possessions. We love those who make us laugh or smile. We hate those who are nasty and mean to us and make us angry or sad. First rule of thinking and taking control of yourself; NO ONE MAKES YOU ANYTHING! YOU DO IT TO YOURSELF!

6

Our emotion buttons are also programmed throughout our lives. We all have certain words or phrases if directed at us press our angry button. Our fear button can easily be pressed by our boss with, "You're fired!" Fear of death is the strongest motivating force that keeps all living things thriving. We all have that record hiding back there with the buttons blacked out so no one can press them. What if you could have someone actually and seriously press those "You're fired!" buttons and you could feel calm and not threatened?

The "You're fired!" record can't be erased. Most all of our records sit intact unless some organic injury or disease attacks them. So how can we keep that "You're fired!" record from being played thereby causing us all sorts of stress and anxiety? The method to employ is called reframing. We know the record is there and we pretty much know the circumstances under which that button will be pressed. If someone else has the power to press the button and you have no way of stopping them from pressing it, what do you do? You are the owner of your jukebox (brain). As the owner you have the right and ability to rearrange your records in any fashion you choose. If the "You're fired!" button is pressed you pretty much have a record in mind right now that you are going to play. Right now we aren't interested in that record, let's think about choosing a different record to play for the "You're fired!" button. There's that word "choose" again.

You can right now choose a different record. How about a nice day at the beach with the sun warm on your body, the sand is warm against your back, the breeze is soft and warm. You hear the seagulls overhead. The waves are slapping on the shore. The sound of children laughing and playing can be heard. You look out on the water and there is large white sailboat slowly passing by. The people on the deck are waving to you yelling to you, you're fired, and you smile and wave back. You take a long cool drink of your drink and set it next to your blanket. You wipe the sweat from your forehead. Ah....now there is a wonderful place all peaceful and calm without a care in the world. What a wonderful record!! You just have to love it when you hear "You're fired!"

This won't change the fact that you will have to find a new job. Of course it can't, however it puts you in a much happier frame of mind than the awful record you had sitting there in the bin before. Now that you are no longer dreading the awful record and can play the one you love you are now free to put all your effort into something positive such as being the best you that you can be to find that next position. "Positive" is the operative word.

I have found that the most important question that you must

9

continually ask yourself all day everyday and be able to answer honestly is; "What positive benefit am I getting out of doing this or thinking this way?" Now we are all placed in "these trying times" each day. Often times we are not able to extricate ourselves from the trying situation such as being in a confrontation with someone at work. It happens all the time to everyone. We all get defensive and the fur flies and we all try to protect ourselves from being "attacked".

The conflicts in interpersonal relationships are so varied and complex no one can predict just how they will play themselves out. We have all had situations were we have done something or said something we regret. No one is perfect. First and foremost you must take 100% personal responsibility for how you feel. NO ONE MAKES YOU ANYTHING! Remember the rule?

10

Even if you are wrongfully accused you can reframe how you think about it. If I screamed at you, "You're an elephant!!!" would you grow a trunk? of course not. Just because someone accuses you of something or calls you something does not make it so. Even in those circumstances where you have been caught making a mistake, which we all do, you can still choose to reframe your thinking to make it a pleasant experience. Critical thinking comes from a complete understanding of just how you think and how you can use the tools of thought to the highest and best use.

I recently lost my mother to Alzheimer's disease. No one would fault me for being sad or carrying on for weeks on end for this "loss". I knew what was coming. I actually know it about everyone, I just don't know when. How do you prepare yourself for this? Reframing is the key tool.

11

We know the "your mother's dead" button will be pressed someday. We have no control over that. But we have complete control as to how we choose to think about that situation. Just was with the "You're fired!" buttons we do the same for your mother's dead. By doing so you may say that you are not allowing for your "natural grieving". I do not subscribe to the notion that grieving is a natural state of mind that is somehow privileged and not to be toyed with as we are to be respectful of the ones we lose through death. I do not disrespect my mother by not falling apart at the seams crying all day and night. In fact I celebrate the fact that I had this wonderful person it my life. I choose to think of when I was a small boy climbing up in her lap and hearing her read me stories. That is the record I choose to play whenever her face is seen in my mind's eye. My "mother" button gives me a feeling of safety and serenity rather than pain.

12

Now on the other side of the equation we can use the same technique to enhance the pleasant things in our lives. Think of some event that you enjoy. Get that picture in your mind and now make the picture sharper, the colors brighter and the sounds even more realistic as if you are right in the midst of it. This can only make your good times even better.

We often times set ourselves up for disappointment. Expectations are just that, expectations and not reality. We all hope for the best outcome and when we fall short of our goal our self esteem goes right down the drain as well. Once again we set up our play list well in advance preparing for the glory and when the failure button got pressed we go right into the dumper. You have every right to set yourself up for success and a favorable outcome. But, you have to also be ready for the downside as well. This is NOT negative thinking, it is preplanning

13

for not choosing an unpleasant result if the failure button is pressed. Sure you'll have every right to be disappointed if things do not work out however you also have every right to be happy no matter what. Doing the reframe ahead of time is what anyone who is successful understands.

Successful people have already gone through the failure and all of the agony that can result from that. They had the forethought and presence of mind to be prepared for as many consequences as possible. The record was changed ahead of time just in case that button gets pushed. With that already taken care of you now can put all your energy and skill into achieving a successful outcome.

Any successful coach has to take into account every possible attack against his team and be ready with some sort of defense. And the coach may actually need backup

14

plans to be ready in case his first
choice fails. Winning generally is the
elimination of circumstances that
cause you to fail. The only way to
overcome the obstacles is to prepare
for them in advance and having all
sorts of options to choose from just
as when you hit your errant golf shot
and yelled "fore". There is an old
adage that "the harder I practice the
luckier I get." There is a lot of truth
to that.

What is the commodity that
winner possess aside from
preparation? I call it tenacity. If you
say you can or you say you
can't...you're right, plain and simple.
If you stop running you will never
finish a race much less win one. Of
course if you do not possess the body
that can perform in the fashion
necessary to win a foot race then you
have to accept the fact that you can't
compete against better bodies. "A
good man knows his limitations" has
a lot of credence however I do not
subscribe to that as my mantra and

15

neither should you. Winners already
have a backup plan in place just in
case they fail. You should too.

Living is just what you think it
is. Your thoughts are your reality. If
you choose to hate you will. If you
choose to love you will. If you choose
any thought it is yours and yours
alone and no matter how much you
desire everyone else to share that
thought you can't do it unless others
choose to think that way as well. The
power of pressing other people's
buttons goes on all day everyday.

Advertisers pay enormous
amounts of cash to convince you to
buy their products. They want to
push your buttons like a slot machine
so your money falls out of your
pocket into theirs. He who is the
cleverest and can do it to the most
people makes the most money. He
who can't convince you to alter your
thinking to give it up voluntarily has
to take it from you. Men like Hitler
convinced millions to give him their

16

country. Those who refused to give it to him were simply eliminated.

By taking 100% responsibility for your own feelings and thinking you can not be influenced by the likes of a Hitler. There may come a time when you are faced with that and you can stand your ground and reframe your mind as necessary. There also may come a time when your refusal to allow the records of submission to be played that the person pressing the button will take up arms against you. Then and only then do you have the final choice physical defense.

Our powers of reason can be used for good or evil which brings me back to the ultimate question of "What positive benefit am I getting out of doing this or thinking this way?" I assume you all want to have a positive life. Of course there are those who will not or cannot subscribe to having a positive outlook or approach to living. That is a shame. However we all must be

17

mindful that these people exist and that they often wish to cause pain in the lives of others.

You will note that I have not said a word about altering anyone's beliefs. Following one's heart is a personal choice and whatever gives one peace and solace is a good thing even if it is contrary to my own. So long as we can all be kind to each other I fail to see where that even becomes an issue. The conflict and evil arises out of being so attached to one's own beliefs that one reaches out to spread their "joy" to the rest of humanity. Your personal relationship with your creator (for lack of a better term) is yours and no one else's.

How you communicate or why you communicate with your creator is your business and no one else's. You do not need to gloat about your relationship as if it is "better" than anyone else's. Living is not a contest. There is no prize waiting for

18

any of us that we can control other than by being kind. It takes far less effort and stress to be kind than it does to be angry. We have a tough enough time keeping ourselves on track than to take on the rest of the world.

Anything beyond simple mathematics is merely an opinion. What one considers good is bad to someone else. Just because a majority of people agree on something being good does not make it so, it is only a majority opinion.

Never fall prey to your own opinion as being the only one. By the same token don't adopt another's opinion for no good reason. As much as you like someone else telling you what is the "right" way to be they don't like it either. We can all coexist without forcing our opinions on others. It is the diversity of life that makes it so enjoyable not the sameness.

19

I had a very good friend who traveled the world. She was frustrated as a young person when she found other cultures doing things "wrong". She made a little note to herself that she kept in her purse and she took it with her whenever she traveled. It said, "You travel to see strange and different things...so don't be surprised if you find them." That was in essence a reframing card. When she hit a snag in a trip she would take that note out and read it to herself out loud. She never had a bad trip again.

We all have thousands of records in our jukebox and how in the world do you rearrange them all to keep your sanity? You do them one at a time as the situations present themselves. Oh you'll have quiet times when you can choose to work on things that are pressing. We all anticipate what may or may not be and we all try to cope. With reframing you are not coping you are taking a positive active role in taking

20

control of living. Living is what you think it is all day everyday. If you want to make a better world, start making you the best you that you can. Let everyone else worry about themselves. You have plenty to keep you busy for a lifetime.

21

APPLYING REFRAMING

Since you now know that you are doing it all to yourself how can you build a strategy to improve your overall performance? Whether winners are actually aware of the technique or not reframing is the method they employ to succeed where others fail. Of course one has to have the skill and talent present in order to perform at any given level. But as we have all seen in countless situations, sports or otherwise, if you take five evenly matched people and give them the exact same task one will no doubt do better than the rest. Look at the Olympics and you will see runners all of whom are nearly identical in size, shape and training yet only one wins the gold. It can't just be luck or overall superiority of the winner. We can take these same athletes and give them the same task on another day and the person who won the first race could be beaten by another runner.

The physical aspects obviously do present the opportunity to give you an edge over others but in many cases physical ability is outshined by one who is of lesser physical prowess. Somewhere in that person's thinking he was able to draw something extra out of himself for a brief moment that gave him the advantage over the physically superior opponent.

There are countless cases where the underdog managed to come from behind and win. Why? The winner actually was able to visualize his success even before his performance. We all have heard of *visualization*. The winner is able to "see" himself succeeding beforehand thereby permitting his brain to automatically start applying the physical aspects to the task.

An example would be a basketball player standing at the free-throw line having to sink a winning basket in a championship game. The player has made that shot thousands of times before. In this circumstance, however, he is faced with the added pressure of the importance of this one particular shot. Picture further that the player has to make this shot on the other team's home court and the crowd is desperately trying everything they can to ensure that he misses this shot.

Pressure is something we apply to ourselves. As mentioned earlier, I deliberately mentioned we are in control of our emotions. The "choke" weighs in everyone's mind from time to time. We all know that choking is a sign of weakness and "causes" failure. Choking is negative thinking that presses all of our failure scenario images. The more important the situation the more apt we are to start playing all of the horror stories in our mind. We literally "see" the demise. As these horrifying images and movies fill out heads we make ourselves physically ill. You have seen people about to take an all important final exam start sweating, panting, and turning red. Some become violently ill even vomiting under this self-imposed "pressure".

These pressure images and movies have been stored long before the event is before you. Just as with the "You're fired!" scenario you have already preprogrammed yourself in the game winning situation "seeing" all of the monsters, hearing the jeers, the booing, the screaming, the horrible cheer when you fail to make that free-throw. As you stand at the line you have already set yourself up to fail. You are playing your own "choke video" as you bounce the ball dreading the shot. Each bounce sounds like thunder in your ears. The sweat is beading on your forehead. You teammates are looking at you with begging looks for you not to blow it. Your breathing is labored. Your heart is pounding. This is all self-imposed.

Any winner foresees these situations. It is inevitable in life that we will be confronted with the game winning scenario.

So what do you do? Since you foresee this scenario there is every good reason to play the winning scenario images and movies when you are in a more relaxed less stressful situation...such as while sitting quietly in your living room. What!? You say. This is an ideal time to gather your thoughts.

Since all of your thinking and reactions are in your head as so many records in a jukebox you have an advantage over pressure situations. You own the jukebox and you control which buttons play which records. If you don't want a certain record played at any given moment when the button is pressed, you merely change the record since the outside world is pressing the buttons.

26

As an example of preprogramming, as I indicated earlier, I was faced with the impending death of my mother. She was terminally ill and beyond hope. The only issue was "when". Knowing full well this circumstance was out of my control and the "she's gone" button would be pushed at any time, I had a choice. I had the power over the records in my head. I could chose which records to play when the "she's gone" button was pressed.

Of course, as it is for everyone, no one wants to lose a loved one. We all dread having that button pushed. But in the real world we do not have the power to control which buttons are pressed or even when they get pressed for the most part.

Since I was now in the position of knowing this event was forthcoming I chose to take a quiet moment when I was alone and rearrange the records. I had the crying and grieving records all set in place ready to play loudly and vividly when the button would be pressed. But by keeping those records and movies in place did what for me? They would make me totally sad, distraught and filled with pain. No one would fault me if I in fact played those records when the button got pressed. But then I asked myself this all important question which I ask myself all day everyday even now; "WHAT POSITIVE BENEFIT AM I GETTING OUT OF DOING THIS OR THINKING THIS WAY?"

The answer was a resounding "NONE!" Would it be disrespectful of me not to fall apart at the death of my mother? Would I be a cold hearted unloving person? Absolutely not, quite the contrary, I would be just the same person I was if I were falling apart at the seams.

28

I chose to rearrange the records.
I didn't even play the grieving records
as I sat there all alone quietly with
my eyes closed contemplating the
variety of circumstances when the
news would come and how it would
be delivered; by phone, in person,
through a relative, a friend or from
the nursing home staff. I had a
pretty good idea of the ways the news
would arrive.

I looked back to a time, a
pleasant wonderful time I had with
my mom. I was three years old. I
had my white t-shirt on and a khaki
shorts on. I had my "Curious George"
book in my little hands and mom was
sitting in our old easy chair smiling at
me. I looked up at her and in my
little voice asked her if she would
read me the story. I saw her smile
and felt her pick me up into her lap
setting the book in front of us and
she opened the book and began to
read. I ran that record over and over
in my mind. I burned it in with the

pictures as clear as I could make them. I made the colors as bright and real as if it was happen right there and then. I was literally living the experience fifty years later just as it had been.

A warm pleasant feeling filled all of my senses. A beautiful smile lit my face. I to this day, when I think of my mom, see only that beautiful scene just like it was happening. I actually become that three year old boy for those moments and my memory of my mom is as pleasant as any memory anyone could picture.

I chose that memory as my record for "she's gone", "mom", "Shirley" and all of the buttons that would bring her to mind. It makes me feel wonderful and it is a tribute to mom that she was so wonderful to me and had such a great impact on me that I can share this powerful tool with you and anyone who is seeking to gain control of their thinking in a positive way.

30

We now go back to our basketball player who is faced with the game winning shot. The player no doubt has practiced shooting free-throws thousands of times. As kids we have all pretended we were in that game winning situation and of course we were able to make that miracle shot or play to win the game. You may think that this would be the record you would want to play when the crucial moment comes. Actually it is even more pointed than pretending. The situation calls for playing the images and movies that depict the exact feelings, sights and sounds we may encounter and then allowing you to actually place yourself into that situation as if it was actually taking place.

As the basketball player you would be filling your senses with all of the surroundings. You first find a quiet place to begin your reframing. The actual amount of time it takes anyone to achieve a reframe is rather quick. Closing your eyes you literally see the surroundings that push the "winning shot" button. The button's name or names would very for each individual but suffice it enough to say that you should anticipate a variety of buttons that may lead to playing the winning scenario thought pattern you require.

As you sit quietly visualizing this scene hone in on not only what you are seeing. You want to feel the ball in your hands. You want to feel the temperature of the surroundings. The lighting becomes more vivid. The sounds of the crowd and the ball hitting the floor as you bounce all fill your senses. You want to create the actual moment.

You hold your head up and breathe deeply as your confidence grows. You see the basket hanging and the light reflecting off of the backboard. It is just waiting for your shot to swish through.

32

You stand confident holding the ball in your hands ready to make this very simple shot that you have made thousands of times before. This is your "winning shot". You take dead aim on the basket and let the ball fly up on its arch and it swishes right through the center of the basket. A smile comes across your face and joy fills your entire body. Every shot is your winning shot now.

You then allow the scene to gently and slowly fade to black and your body relaxes totally. You have achieved your goal for your winning shot and you are prepared to bring this new movie into your thinking anytime you need a winning shot whether it is the first shot of the season or just practicing in your driveway.

Rerun this movie in your mind over and over again. Brighten the colors. Make them softer...sharper...you are in total control of this movie and no one else can change it. Take full command of the situation. You can change it in any positive way you choose. There are no rules. The only consequence is that your performance is brought to an even higher level.

You can use this same technique for any situation you may encounter in your life. It is not just for sports but for all of your interaction with the world around you.

Winners anticipate trying situations. They deliberately take the time to foresee the scene and condition themselves with the thoughts that allow the body to function appropriately for the given task.

Of course even the best of players even using these techniques will still not perform perfectly each and every time they are called upon to make that winning shot.

34

What can you do when you do miss that shot? The humiliation, disappointment, shame, anger, embarrassment...all of these self-imposed emotions can fill your head so quickly you will not have time to think. The winner prepares for these failures as well. This is not negative thinking. Quite the contrary, it is positive thinking that will allow you to get beyond any mistakes so you can apply your thought processes to winning scenarios rather than replaying over and over the failures and mistakes.

The adage that we all learn from our mistakes does NOT mean that we punish ourselves repeatedly for a short coming. Failures are opportunities for improvement and growth. However, that is not going to help you at the fatal moment when that basketball bounces off of the rim and the game goes down the drain. Anyone who has been through a similar situation know that anyone who reminds you that "Oh, its okay, we all learn from our mistakes." is someone looking to get punched square in the nose. Those sports reporters interviewing the players in the loser's locker room know they are taking their dental work in their own hands and tread lightly.

Now if you look back at one of those post-game interviews in the loser's locker room where the athlete being interviewed has been a winner far more times than not you will most likely see a player who is not mortified by the situation and has a logical explanation for why his performance was not peaking at that moment.

You'll say, "Well that doesn't change the fact that they lost." Of course it doesn't change that. But it does change how that athlete thinks of himself. He is not dwelling on failure. What he is thinking about at the moment most likely has absolutely nothing with what just happened. Even if the player isn't being interviewed the winner is not beating up on himself focusing on every little mistake he made or bad call that could have gone the other way. THERE IS NO POSITIVE BENEFIT IN PLAYING THE BLAME GAME.

The winner has probably switched movies to something far more pleasant, and rightly so. Your mental state is your choice, period. Moaning and groaning is one way of thinking if you so choose. But then you must ask yourself, "What positive benefit am I getting out of this?" That is indeed the most important question a person can ask himself.

If you happen to be in that situation where you have just lost the big game, lost money on a real estate deal or some other major disappointing scenario, would it not be smarter if you had prepared yourself in advance for that event? Of course it would have. But then again we all say we don't want to jinx ourselves by preparing for our

concession speech in advance
because by doing so we are creating a
negative outlook or inviting bad
karma. I would disagree completely
with that assumption.

A winner prepares himself for
failures. Any astronaut will spend
countless weeks and months
preparing for the every conceivable
failure anyone can think of. The
astronaut will rehearse thousands of
scenarios and protocols that may be
needed should a failure occur. Only a
fool would enter into a situation
without foreseeing and preparing for
a glitch.

As a trial lawyer I had to
prepare a case not just hoping
everything would go totally in my
favor. I had to anticipate every
possible situation that may go against
me and find a solution IN ADVANCE
that I could apply quickly to
minimize the damages. No one
should approach any one situation
strictly from an offense point of view.

We all need a good defense. In many cases it is that great defense that actually gets us to our goal. Succeeding is not doing everything perfectly…it is making the fewest mistakes and making appropriate adjustments along the way to reach the ultimate goal.

A true winner studies the situation before jumping in. Football teams spend weeks analyzing film footage of opposing teams in hopes of finding out their plays.

So there is no reason when we find ourselves in the loser's locker room that we can't be happy and positives. This situation is no different than my anticipation of my mom's death and having the foresight and ability to prepare myself for that. You as a winner must be prepared to lose as well.

And you don't have to feign being happy about your loss. You do no service to yourself to put on the "hair shirt" and punish yourself for losing. There is no reason you can't sit down and prepare yourself for a nice Caribbean cruise frame when the final buzzer sounds and you head for the loser's locker room. You are not minimizing the loss or showing any disrespect for your teammates by having a pleasant demeanor following a loss. You have every good reason to be happy no matter what. Sure if you lose a big game you would have every good reason to be angry or even throw a temper tantrum to show everyone just how important that loss was. But you are not really showing any sort of respect for yourself or the others around you by blowing your top. The question is valid; "What positive benefit am I getting out of doing this or thinking this way?"

You answer, "I'm just letting it out! It's not healthy to keep it balled up inside! You just don't understand! This was it! This was my chance!" Well, you have every right to do that and no one will fault you for it. Some may say there is something wrong with you if you don't go ballistic. I disagree.

We have all heard, "If life gives you lemons make lemonade." And we usually respond to that, "Easier said than done." I submit to you that it is in fact far EASIER DONE THAN SAID!

Using these reframing tools you have the ability to reprogram yourself to become a more confident, less stressed and all 'round happier person. And it only takes a small amount of time to make significant changes in your thought patterns. You are in control yet most people either don't realize it, refuse to take charge or are lacking the tools to change. As we progress through this book you will see a number of examples of real life situations which can be reframed quite easily permitting you to not just cope but to become proactive in all aspects of your life. You can take command of how you feel and develop the confidence and skills to be your own "spin doctor" quickly and efficiently.

You have by now seen that serious horrible situations can be taken head on without much difficulty. You can also maintain this control at will. You have learned that you do it all to yourself. Learning that lesson alone is worth its weight in gold. Perfecting the skills of active positive thinking allows you to maximize your enjoyment of every moment you have.

42

How important is this?

Assume for a moment that you knew that tonight at midnight you would die comfortably and painlessly, but die nonetheless. Knowing this and that you only have this tiny amount of time left stop reading and look at the clock. Add up the minutes you have left until midnight.

We are conditioned to sell our time being employed for a given hourly rate or salary. We made a conscious choice at that time to sell a portion of our life for a price.

Knowing what few minutes you have left now in our pretend scenario, how much is your time worth now?

Your entire value system was hopefully just turned on its ear. THAT IS HOW PRECIOUS YOUR TIME REALLY IS!

If I were selling tickets to 12:30, what would you be willing to pay for that extra 30 minutes? You immediately see just how precious your life is. Wasting what little time you have being sad, angry, disappointed, frustrated...you name it, is really a tragic waste indeed. What I endeavor to do here is give you some tools which will allow you to maximize your enjoyment of the remainder of your time. BEING MISERABLE IS TRAGIC. Life doe not have to be tragic. You are entitled to be happy just as you are entitled to be miserable...it is your CHOICE.

No matter what life presents you have to make a choice as to how you perceive it. Life is a state of mind. The state of mind you choose dictates how you feel and how you perform. Certainly most of what life presents to you is out of your control. If you can't control the stimulus you can always control your perception of it.

44

Many of these perceptions or states of mind have been preprogrammed into you either consciously or unconsciously.

Taking an infant at birth it has no preconceived notions about what anything is or has an opinion about anything beyond eating and sleeping. Gradually the infant is bombarded with all sorts of stimuli, some of it good and some of it bad but for all intent and purposes completely new and unknown. The environment around the infant will have a dramatic affect on what perceptions are rewarded by others and which ones are not.

We all seek safety. Being safe is the prime objective and motivation for all animals, man included. While we go about our lives indicating all sorts of things and events as being "important" the most important of all is being free from harm. Anything that threatens your safety will no doubt be met head on with some sort of attack or defense on your part. It is just the natural order of us all.

We seek basic safety; food, air, water, shelter and clothing. The degrees of comfort and the levels of societal pecking order tend to cover up the basics for most of us. If you are reading this most likely your basic survival needs are already being met. It is important to keep in mind though that these primal instincts of survival are very powerful and will cause you to have involuntary reactions. We have all experienced that shot of adrenalin throughout veins when taken by surprise. We all have also done or said things out of anger without thinking. With the tools for reframing you can take control and prepare in advance for any situation you can think of ahead of time.

It is clear that we can't spend our entire time preparing for each and every encounter life presents us. For the winners the focus is on the ultimate goal he wants to achieve. A winner develops a road map, if you will, and then sets himself on that path toward the goal. If you have ever played a video game where you have to reach the castle and save the princess or some other such goal, you know there are many obstacles that are placed in your way. Overcoming these obstacles is the key to your success.

Using the video game as an example here, more than likely when you first played the game you just turned it on and started frantically pressing buttons trying to figure out just how the game works and you end up getting "killed" a thousand times in the process. Few of us actually sit down and read the instructions before jumping in and flailing away.

Unfortunately for many of us we approach our real life pretty much in this same fashion. Then when we get clobbered by the demons and traps set for us along the way we get frustrated and for most of us ultimately give up.

For most everything you wish to achieve in life there is a strategy on how to reach that goal. Some things are far more difficult than others and require a great amount of skill and training. Others can be quite simple. We all tend to revert back to the simple less difficult things and we tend to seek a comfort level for ourselves which is why everyone does different things. Your personal tastes will determine what you find pleasant. You ability to untangle the strategies for various activities will determine what you do.

You may love to listen to music. However, in order to create music or play an instrument requires training, skill and a lot of practice. If you possess the basic body parts to play an instrument your success in playing that instrument are determined by those factors. While some are indeed "gifted" in certain areas, there are plenty of people who become extremely proficient at playing an instrument. This is true with most every discipline in life; mathematics, art, science, medicine, law, sports, and any other thing you can think of. With all things being equal between two people doing the same thing what makes one person excel in that field beyond the other? I would submit that all of the training, skill and practice have an awful lot to do with that. However, the person who ultimately wins (all things being equal otherwise) has a mindset that the other person didn't have during the competition.

Not only did the winner excel at the physical aspects, he also excelled at how he thought his way through it. This command of the thought processes is what gives you the edge over others. You learned the strategies and apply them in a fashion that others don't.

THE "LUCK" FACTOR

If you ask a great golfer who is about average in skill level relative to his opponents how it is he was able to win he no doubt will say, "I was lucky." I sincerely doubt that "luck" had anything to do with his success, or yours for that matter. Gary Player's famous quote still rings true; "The harder I practice, the luckier I get."

Many still believe in luck. Las Vegas was built on it. But, if luck was a tangible for you why aren't you the one owning all of those luxurious hotel/casinos? If you honestly believe that luck has anything to do with your performance you might as well stop reading right now and cast your fate to the wind.

As best as anyone can tell, luck is a superstition and is used to explain away the improbable. Winners do not ascribe to luck being the determinative factor for their performance. Luck is a term used to discount someone's achievement which was due to his training, skill and mental fortitude. The "miracle" shot, kick or base hits in life come from applying what you have in the best manner you can at the moment you are performing. Stealing someone's spotlight is all luck is used for. Relying on luck gets you nowhere. Luck has no place in the mind of a winner as a true component for success. When you succeed *you* should get credit. Enough about luck, for winners there is no such thing.

51

RUNNING YOUR BRAIN

Knowing how to access your records and movies is imperative for success. You access your memories by the way you move your eyes. We've all heard the teacher say to a student stumped by a question saying, "The answer isn't on the ceiling!" Actually...it probably is!

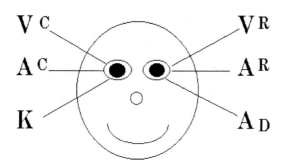

EYE MOVEMENTS -- NORMAL RIGHT HANDED PERSON

VC = visual image constructed
VR = visual image remembered
AC = audio constructed
AR = audio remembered
K = feelings
AD = audio dialog [*1]

The chart above is looking at a normal right handed person. The way he moves his eyes accesses the information indicated as to where he looks.

People generally look…
up and to your right, *VC*, when thinking about a remembered image (your mom) up and left, *VR*, when

constructing an image (your mom standing on her head), directly right, *AC*, for a remembered sound (your mom's voice), directly left, *AR*, for a constructed sound (your mom saying she's included you in her will), down and to your right, *K*, when having an internal dialog with themselves ("Boy, I hate Aunt Sal") and; down and left, *AD*, when experiencing feelings (experiencing how you really feel about Aunt Sal).

You can start using these eye movements to start accessing your memory banks right now. If I ask you, "What color was your first bike?" Notice where your eyes just moved, they went up and to your left (if you're right handed).

More important here is that you probably haven't thought about your first bike in decades yet in a matter of seconds you were able to see it in your mind's eye. The term "photographic memory" was not selected by accident.

54

If you are trying to remember something your saw you look up to your right and WAIT! Your brain takes time to find what you're looking for.

Those things you access the least or have the least amount of impact on you are stored far back and take a little time to come to the forefront. The keys are YOUR EYE MOVEMENT *AND* WAITING.

You have to have patience and trust the fact that the information is indeed stored inside your brain. We all have had the experience when someone asked you to recall something and you gave up only finding out at 2 am that the answer just "happened" to come to you. That was not the case. You quit. The answer was there. You just ran out of patience or in the case of an examination, you ran out of time.

You should practice using your eye movements to start recalling all sorts of things. It is fun and extremely important. And like everything else you do, the more you practice it, the better you get at it.

Your thought process is very closely tied with your physiology. A dog senses your fear: how did he know if you didn't tell him. If a friend is depressed, most of us can tell without even talking with them. We pick up clues from their body: slumped shoulders, eyes downcast, head down, lack of animation (and in extreme cases, a loaded pistol held to the head). *Sensory acuity* takes these observations beyond the more obviously recognizable clues and uses the physical feedback in addition to someone's words to gain as much from communication as possible.

If you are depressed your first step out of it is to change your posture. You sit up straight, hold your head up, take deep breaths and most importantly SMILE. We don't smile enough.

To recap;

Your *eye movement* accesses your memories,

Your *posture* sets your mood.

SMILE.

These simple tools will give you the power you are looking for.

57

Knowing what type of person you are is all important as to how you process information. Winners choose to take in information in the most efficient and effective way possible. Take a look at the following examples and see which one fits your best.

Visual: Yep, looks good to me.
Auditory: I've been hearing good things about it.
Kinesthetic: I feel good about the whole project.
Olfactory: Smells like a winner to me.
Gustatory: I can taste the victory.

One or more of these fits you and how you learn things. Some of us do far better by having things shown to us while others need to be told. Some of us are hands on kind of people. Whichever you happen to be it is in your best interest to learn which ways are the best ways to teach you new things.

By the same token, knowing this also tells you how you access

58

memories as well. If you are a visual
person you are more adept at
recalling things you saw and you had
best be looking up and to your right
an awful lot to find what you're
looking for. The same holds true if
you are auditory etc...

While these things appear to be
simplistic they are indeed the steps
to power and building yourself into a
winner. You will be using these tools
for the rest of your life. Running
your brain is a good thing.

On the other side of the coin
regarding eye movement you can use
this information to find out how
someone else is accessing
information. Poker players are
masters at reading a person's eyes
and mannerisms. The oil sheiks wear
sunglasses during negotiations so the
other person can read them.

As a trial lawyer I used a witness' eye movements to find out whether he was actually recalling something he had seen or something he was told he had seen. This was extremely beneficial in fraud cases where even their attorney was involved in fabricating stories. By asking pointed questions where I suspected the witness had been told what to say I would carefully watch his immediate eye movement to determine if it was an audio constructed (AC) movement as opposed to a visual remembered (VR) movement. If I detected an AC movement I knew he didn't have an actual visual recollection. The question could be as simple as "What color was the other person's hair?" Even a blank stare was a dead give away when the witness had never seen the other person.

As you can see these tools are extremely valuable and far reaching in their application. As you begin using these methods you will see a

60

change in how you deal with yourself
and the world around you. You will
begin to have a sense of control and
power not over others or the things
around you, but rather over you and
how you choose to feel about it all.

STRATEGIES

A strategy is the internal
thought process of the model: a
sequence of representations the
person goes through in order to
achieve their outcome. A strategy has
three crucial aspects:
* The representation systems used.
* The distinctions within the
representation systems
(submodalities)
* The sequence of the steps.

There are some principles of well
formed strategies too: it should have
an outcome, and it should involve all
three main representational systems
(Visual, Auditory and Kinesthetic).
There should be no loops without an

exit point and there should be at least one step that relates to the outside world.

This all sounds quite complicated but let's break it into simple English. A model is like sheet music is to music. It is a representation of notes that can be played on a variety of instruments while maintaining the basic structure of the song. A model is an overall map of a given phenomenon. It should also contain explicit information of what steps should be taken in what order to obtain a given outcome. A model cannot be proved true or false, only that it works or not.

So if a musician in Australia has the same sheet music as a musician in New York the two can use the sheet music (model) to play the same tune.

62

The same holds true for most everything we learn to do. So a winning athlete learns the basic model of throwing or catching a ball. He learns the basics of his sport and then tries to master each skill in a physical sense.

What is offered here is a basic model, or strategy, for running your brain. You take these basic tools and put them to use as best you can until, through practice, you begin to master the techniques. The great part of be able to use reframing is that the more you do it the better you get at and as an added bonus...you feel great!

Human beings are somewhat more complicated. You cannot take a skill out of context without changing the skill. If you model Einstein's thought process, you will not become another Einstein, however you will be able to enrich and broaden your own thinking using his strategies.

63

What this means is that you can
use the same strategies but it is still
you doing it and not Einstein. Taking
Einstein's strategies to the next level
would be you actually creating new
strategies out of his.

Submodalities
Submodalities are the distinctions we
make within a representational
system. For instance, brightness,
distance and motion are
submodalities. Some, such as
direction, are common to all
representational systems.
Submodalities may be discontinuous,
that is on or off, for example
associated or dissociated. A memory
cannot be both at once. Or they may
be continuous or analogical, varying
on a sliding scale, such as brightness
or volume.

When you sit down and start
your reframing you will actually be
substituting one record for another,
or mixing up your jukebox.

64

It is imperative that you be mindful that your changes will be more dramatic and more permanent if you are selective with your substitutions. You are making these changes to make yourself feel better. You don't want to haphazardly select records or movies that are going to cause you harm or a complete irrational response to a given stimulus. You should be subtle.

Furthermore, there is no need for you to go to the opposite ends of the emotional spectrum such as going from a completely miserable thought pattern to one of total ecstasy. The goal is to even your feeling out and not get carried away.

I had a good friend who gave me some excellent advice many years ago. He told me, "If you want to be a millionaire, go find a millionaire, follow him around, dress like him, read what he reads, eat what he eats, copy everything he does and before you know it you'll be a millionaire too."

At first I laughed at that advice. But then it dawned on me that the "millionaire" model was a great idea. Athletes "copy" other athletes. Basketball players try to mimic the stars and it holds true for all sports. To be the greatest golfer you learn the basic techniques and adapt those models and strategies to your own situation and try to be the best "you" that you can be. The key is to realize that you are becoming the best "you" not the next whomever the star is you want to be.

It is to your benefit to model yourself after someone who is doing exactly what you would like to do. Of course if you happen to be 5' 4" you will be hard pressed to mimic a professional basketball star. But there is no reason that you can't become the very best 5' 4" basketball player in the entire world!

66

My mother used to tell me she didn't care what I became when I grew up. She just wanted me to be the best "whatever" I could possibly be. "If you're a ditch digger, be the best ditch digger you can be!" Those words echo in my mind as if she just said them this instant.

Using someone else as your model is fine. However, getting that person's thought patterns may not actually be what you need to achieve similar physical results. Every person is different. Since we are different there really is no way to be a 100% copy of someone else. Actually you really wouldn't want to be a carbon copy of anyone. So it should be your goal to select several different models and then choose those aspects from each model that suits you best.

Once you have your models in place you need to burn into your muscle memory just what it is that these people are doing physically and adapt those particular motions to your body.

If you are modeling a businessman then you would be mimicking as closely as you can what the businessman is doing as part of his successful routine. If he is reading certain newspapers or articles, you should be too.

Your mission is to learn as much about your models as you can. You must be very keen on identifying those strategies that your model uses to achieve his successful results. You are constantly a student of your work. You are never satisfied with where you are at any given moment. You are constantly looking for new avenues, strategies and even new model from which to work.

68

Reframing Steps

1. Choose a topic area where you want to perform better.

2. Put yourself into a light trance.

3. a. Tell your unconscious mind to review every time you've done the activity.

   b. Tell it to review the scenes from the inside [first person point of view], and from several vantage points.

   c. Tell it to review the sights, sounds, and feelings.

4. a. As it reviews, ask it to note the ten BEST times you ever did the activity.

   b. Tell it to find out what those ten times have IN COMMON that the other times don't have. It might be something physical, something visual, something auditory, a state of mind, etc.

5. Tell it to begin doing those common things more and more in the future, and monitor the results to find out if those are the crucial distinctions.

6. Tell yourself to drop into a deep trance and do those instructions.

Do this daily for a few weeks. At that point, do it again, but for the "topic," choose "learning to learn." That will have your unconscious mind find out how/when/where it learns best. After you've mastered that, enrich step #3 by having your unconscious mind review other people who are superb at, and review THOSE PEOPLE being excellent from within their bodies.

Using this step by step method you will be training your mind to burn in winning strategies. You are visualizing and creating records and movies of the successful scenes that you wish to recreate.

70

For example, make a picture of someone you love in your mind.

Now, make the colors more intense and notice how it affects your response to it.

Now make it black and white and notice your response.

Return it to its original shades and hue and bring the image closer.

Now move it farther out.

Return the picture to its original state, noticing how each of those experiments affected your response.

Submodalities are the fine tuning to your representations and can be used to create powerful changes.

The interesting thing to note here is that once you understand that **you** create your internal world, you realize ***you can change it.***

71

We represent the world using the visual (images), auditory (sounds), kinesthetic (touch and internal feelings), gustatory (tastes) and olfactory (smells) senses.

We *picture* ourselves lying on a sunny beach, *hear* the voice of the lifeguard yelling, *feel* the sensation only sand in your bathing suit can produce, *taste* the soggy egg salad sandwiches we brought for lunch and *smell* the aroma of the surf wafting into our nostrils.

Our thinking consists of these images, sounds, feelings and usually to a lesser extent, tastes and smells. Our experiences have been recreated through these senses in our memories and shape our capabilities and beliefs.

You must become a student of yourself. When you become intimately familiar with all of your senses you are in a better position to control your thinking. The scenes

72

you create are yours for the choosing.
No one does it "to" you. You do it to
yourself. The next time you are
looking for someone to blame for
how badly you feel...grab a mirror!

73

EXERCISE

Think of a time when you were having an unpleasant conflict with someone else (if you've never had one, call me and I'll yell at you).
This can be your;
husband,
child,
business associate
or
ANYONE.

Re-experience this situation (I know, I know but we're going to make it better soon). Notice the other person's reactions, their physical posture, and gestures.

Clear that image away and now, re-experience the situation as the other person.

Using the information you gathered in the first stage, step into their shoes and imagine as you progress through the experience, what their feelings and attitudes are.

74

After you have processed any new knowledge gained through that experience, you can clear that image away and now,

Re-experience the experience from no one's point of view. In other words, watch the both of you from a neutral space. Notice any new information gained by this new perspective.

Now what? Well, the information you've gathered from these different points of view have enormous value. You can now perceive how others see you and how an entire situation can be viewed from a neutral position. Instead of one way of experiencing the world, you have **Three-3-III** and you are better able to empathize with others and make more objective decisions. Having all this information readily available is the basis for wisdom.

75

Warning:

While this is a very useful way to experience and gather information about the world, realize that these are your guesses as to how others are feeling and one should *test the waters* before jumping in.

As you can see these techniques work in all aspects of your interpersonal relationships as well. There is no reason you can't use these techniques to your advantage both on and off the field.

TAKING "YOU" OUT OF CONFLICTS

We all have conflicts with others. So long as there are two people left on earth there will be conflict. Once again I will repeat the all important question; "What positive benefit am I getting out of doing this or thinking this way?"

We love to win. Winning arguments seems to be a source of great enjoyment and frustration for people. An opinion is like a belly button and everybody has one. So what do you do when you get into an argument? How important is "winning" and argument to you? To say it better; "What positive benefit am I getting out of winning this argument?"

Winning an argument may not be your goal. Defining your goal in a conflict is all important. Are you out simply to humiliate someone? Are you seeking to just be "right"? Are you trying to educate someone? Are they trying to educate you?

Hurting someone else for the sake of "winning" an argument serves no positive benefit to anyone. Revenge is of no use.

In many cases, some people aren't looking for an argument at all and are simply venting. So how do you identify what the other person is feeling? How do you determine what it is they are trying to tell you? Perhaps they aren't interested in your opinion.

In those situations where someone is angry with you (you'll know that one for sure) the last thing you want to do is immediately go on the defensive. An angry person is almost impossible to reason with so there is no sense wasting your efforts trying to talk them out of it with reason. We all know that that doesn't work.

What should you do? Your coach is fuming because you lost the game or blew a play. You already know that he is angry and you are disappointed for "dropping the ball" so to speak. Making excuses for your set back won't change the fact that the play was a bust. You don't want your coach yelling at you but you know you can't avoid this scenario from time to time. So if you already know that this will be happening to you in the future you need to set a new frame around that scenario as demonstrated above.

This is only a partial solution for the conflict. Sure you may feel better, but what about the coach? The way to deal with someone who is out of control angry is to eliminate blame from the conversation. You need to *reflective listen*.

What is reflective listening?
Reflective listening is listening for
what the other person is feeling and
not what he is saying.

Example;

Coach, "I can't believe you screwed
that up! What's wrong with you! You
stink on ice! I should throw you off
the team!!!!"

What is the coach feeling? You
of course feel totally attacked and
threatened. The coach is angry,
disappointed and frustrated. So what
would be a reflection of what the
coach is feeling?

You, "You're angry."

Coach, "Damn right I'm angry! You
screwed up, you loser!"

You, "You're disappointed." Coach,
"Hell yes I'm disappointed." You,
"You're frustrated since the play was
busted."

This is simplistic but the point is that the coach will know that you have heard what he is feeling and interpersonal communication is about expressing *feelings*. Of course you can't re-run the play. But the coach knows you understand what he is feeling.

This would be the same if your spouse or best friend was angry and upset with you. Whether their reasons for being angry and upset are legitimate are NOT the issue. To them the issue is crystal clear and they are not open to reason or ready to hear any explanations until they are finished making their point. For some people it may take a while to get it all out. In the mean time, you do just what you did with the coach; you reflect back the person's feelings rather than start World War III over something that may not be all that important in the long run.

81

By mastering reflective listening you will be less frustrated in conflicts. Attacks on you, legitimate or not, can not be resolved until the parties are ready to speak rationally. Your goal at the outset of a conflict is to determine what the other person is feeling and then reflect back to them that you hear their *feelings*. Once the smoke clears and the other person realizes that you understand their *feelings* they will be more open to a rational discussion. You have not thrown gas on the fire and showed enough restraint to allow the person to vent and further showed your compassion for the other person's feelings. What else are friends for?

You may end up learning something about yourself that you didn't know that has been upsetting the other person and that something may well be what you are open to changing. Don't jump to conclusions. **When you are talking you are not listening and if you aren't listening you aren't learning.**

82

"I" Statements

Many times all we are looking for is support and reassurance. We all have fears and apprehensions. We all hate when others try to tell us what is good or bad for use. No one wants to be told what to do even if what we are doing is wrong or even dangerous. While you can't control someone else from telling you what's good for you, you can learn an effective technique to deal with these sorts of situations.

If you want to be a winning coach you are definitely going to need to learn how to get people to do what they are told and motive them to perform at their best. Screaming and yelling does little for a coach or a player. Showing respect for others is the quickest way to have it heaped back on top of you.

83

The following are examples of what you probably have been doing and what reframing your statement as an "I" statement can do. The preference for an "I" statement as opposed to a "You" statement is readily apparent and far more effective.

You statements	*"I" statements*
Blaming. "You make me so mad."	"I feel angry when you ____." Or, "I have chosen to let it bother me when you ____."
Judging or labeling. "You are an inconsiderate, hostile, arrogant creep."	"I feel betrayed when you criticize me in front of others."
Accusing. "You don't give a damn about me!"	"I feel neglected when you avoid me."
Ordering. "You shut up!"	"I feel annoyed when you call me names and make fun of

85

	me."
Questioning. "Are you always this flirtatious?" or "Why did you do that? I feel like slapping your face."	"I really feel insecure about our relationship when you flirt."
Arguing. "You don't know what you are talking about."	"I feel convinced it is this way."
Sarcasm. "Of course, you are an expert!"	"I would like you a lot more if you were a bit more humble."
Approving. "You are wonderful." "You are attractive."	"I really am impressed with your _____ and besides I like you. I am attracted to you."

86

Disapproval. "You are terrible."	"I feel crushed when you seem only interested in spending my money."
Threatening. "You had better..."	"I'd like it if you'd ..."
Moralizing. "You ought to ..."	"I think it would be fair for you to..."
Treating. "You need to rest and..."	"I'd like to be helpful to you."
Supporting. "It will get better."	"I'm sorry you feel ..."
Analyzing. "You can't stand to leave your mother!"	"I'm disappointed that you are so reluctant to leave..."

87

The differences are like night and day and the results are far more positive. That is what you are seeking in all you do, *POSITIVE BENEFITS.*

The use of "I" puts the onus on you and not the other person. You are essentially relaying your feelings back to the person rather than attacking them and putting them on the immediate defensive. There is no positive benefit in accelerating a situation into a major conflict. If the other person is unable to put the fire out then it is up to you to take control of the situation by ending the contest and get back to understanding what you and the other person are feeling. INTERPERSONAL COMMUNICATION IS ABOUT *FEELINGS.*

You should always be looking for opportunities to use "I" statements. It is far too easy to slip back into the confrontation mode of

88

conversation which leads to frustration and failure. Enlightening your friends about your newly found "I" statements can only make your communications better.

89

Recap, when to consider "I" statements:

Any time you want to share your feelings or desires in a frank, unthreatening, undemanding way. When you are trying to disclose more about yourself to build a relationship.

Any time stress is experienced in a relationship, especially if you are feeling angry or dissatisfied or if the other person is resistive to changing in response to your requests or demands.

If both parties have problems, i.e. both of you can take turns giving "I" statements and giving empathy responses.

If the other person is using a lot of "you" (blaming, critical) statements, try to translate them into "I" statements and empathize with the accuser's feelings.

90

ANCHORING

No doubt you have heard of Pavlov's dog being trained to salivate at the sound of a bell. That sound was the "anchor" that triggered the dog's reaction. Anchoring is important for a winner to create such automatic reactions under specific circumstances. Just as we discussed earlier about the basketball player having to make the winning shot, he developed an anchor to set all of his physical attributes necessary to sink that winning basket.

It is easier to learn how to create an anchor by actually doing it. So I will run through the steps of creating an anchor here as I create one for myself.

First you need to choose a state or resource that you would like to have instant access to. I, like many people, am not too comfortable with public speaking... so let's use confidence. Confidence would be the required resource that would greatly aid my public speaking problem.

Next I think back to a time when I was extremely confident.... OK, got one! .....I am 14 yrs old at the local fair ground about to win a huge soft toy for someone I have had a crush on since primary school.... To win I need to hit three playing cards with darts, I have always been a good darts thrower and very confident I am going to win... which I did, and my skill was rewarded by my first real kiss! My confidence bucket was well and truly overflowing!

Before I reach the peak of the experience (that's the point when the last dart hit the board and I knew I had won... and the resulting prize!!) I need to choose my anchors. Kinesthetically, I choose to clench my left fist (I would choose both fists but I might be carrying something when I need to activate the trigger!) as an auditory cue I will say the word CONFIDENT is a positive and confident tone. For a visual cue I have selected the image of an audience looking up at me, it is an easy visualization and is likely to be present when I need my confidence boost the most!

With my anchors ready I get back to the fair ground, really getting into it and seeing through those eyes and feeling those emotions as I did on that day... My confidence builds as I run through the chain of events. As the last darts hits I am feeling more confident then any other time in my life! The moment the confident feeling hits its peak... (Oh. she's about to kiss me!) I fire all three anchors at once! "CONFIDENT!"

Now that the anchor is installed I break the state, by walking around and thinking of unrelated thoughts etc. Next I trigger the anchor to see if it worked....

Give me a second... (Clenching left fist visualizing the audience and using that same positive confident tone... "CONFIDENT!" Excellent!! I do feel confident, and oddly enough the thought of having to give a speech is actually exciting, not scary!

So, that's how you can create an anchor! Play with it and enjoy it, once you have created your anchor test it out. If it is not as powerful as you hoped you can simply repeat the process, or, try stacking many resources on one anchor. Think of times when you have been happy, excited, confident, brave etc., Associate with the memory as described above and really feel those positive feelings come flooding back. At the peak of the experience fire off your anchor, using the same anchor to stack many states is an extremely powerful process.

To collapse an anchor you would follow a different procedure. You must first identify the problem state, and decide upon an alternative positive state to take its place. You then create the positive state anchor in the usual way. Once complete you must break state and then create an anchor for the negative state, so that both states are anchored and can be triggered easily.

After breaking state again you need to fire each state in turn without breaking state between. Finally fire both anchors at once... this will cause a little confusion while your physiology attempts to achieve both states simultaneously, now break the negative state but keep the positive state going.

To test the success of the collapse break state and fire the negative anchor, the result should be a neutral state, somewhere between the two states. If the negative state persists positive anchors can be stacked on the same anchor and the procedure repeated.

It is important to create a very powerful positive state, even if this requires stacking states together, as the positive state must be stronger than the negative state to collapse the negative anchor.

"State" consists of your mental state. The state you wish to change is manipulated using anchors. Anchors are basically "buttons" as in "She's pushing my buttons." Just as the "fore!" anchor or button works for golfers, you can choose anchors to create the state you wish to have.

You now know that you can look back at your past to find your own anchors which you have used to "psych" yourself up and had successful results. Many baseball players and also golfers go through a routine before every swing. If something disturbs them during that routine they will actually stop the process and start over right from the being. Some people call these

routines superstition but actually
they are the buttons the players press
to get themselves in the proper state
to perform at their best.
[See:
http://www.watchtheskies.co.uk/nlp-
hypnosis/designing-states/]

THE "ZONE"

We have all heard of the "zone". Athletes tell us on those occasions when their performance was nearly perfect they weren't even aware of what they were doing, "it just happened". After a lot of thinking and analysis regarding my own personal situation in having to deal with massive amounts of pain each day I actually and intentionally place myself in my own "zone", if you will, each day and maintain it almost all day. I am reminded of the words of Scarlet O'Hara in Gone With the Wind where she would say, "I won't think about that right now. I'll think about that tomorrow."

As a bit of background I should tell you that I was in an "end of life" program and in hospice care suffering from cancer followed by a massive stroke. I still carry my funeral card to this day. I was told there was no hope and sent home to die. In October of 2003 I suffered a massive stroke which left me in a coma and paralyzed.

I was in a state of total confusion and helpless. I was consciously unaware of my surroundings even though, they tell me I was able to converse though I made little sense most of the time. My memory is pretty much a complete blur from about August 2003 to the end of January 2004. I do have short 2 or 3 frame movie clips of being in nursing homes. Being run over by an electric wheel chair and falling out of bed.

To pain from the cancer alone was unbearable even with Morphine. The pain and suffering were exacerbated by the conflicts I was having with my own faith and spirituality since I had already died twice during cancer surgery April 1, 2003 and there was no "light"!

My hospice counselor and I had many long discussions about my situation and as I had a fairly extensive education the other counselors were reluctant to take me on. He and I discussed what it was like lying there helpless with no hope of ever returning to health. The fear of what was about to be and the finality of it all was crazy-making for sure. Yet, though it all I was able to cope. I was hallucinating and the images were just as real as anything to me.

My brain was doing all it could to take my conscious mind off of the life ending issue and trying desperately to get me into the state of appreciating what I did have and not what I was about to lose.

The main lesson I learned was that I was losing nothing. My perception of life and reality was a state of mind and that state of mind was of my choosing or the result of some mind altering drug. So it occurred to me that perhaps I could choose not to think about the pain or the horror of losing my life just as Scarlet O'Hara had done with her situation.

That sound silly and virtually impossible as some stupid movie scenario but then again what did I have to lose in trying? All was already lost according to the experts.

I was alone most of the time lying in bed staring at the ceiling writhing in pain feeling sorry for myself, cursing God and the world for dealing me this rotten hand. Then one afternoon I asked myself, "What positive benefit am I getting out of doing this or thinking this way?" The answer was obviously "none". But I couldn't change the fact that my body was rotting away and the pain was horrific. The episodes of hours of projectile vomiting and vibrating out of control were almost a daily occurrence. How does one overcome this sort of horror? And even today a few years out of the nursing home still hobbling about in severe pain with residual brain damage that affects my physical abilities (more on the right side)…how do I deal with waking up each morning caught by surprise with all of that pain out of control? The simple answer is "see above".

I put myself in the "no pain zone" every morning. My wife can attest to the severity of it all and the process takes a minute or two. But, as with all skills, since I have been doing it for years now, I can get myself to a manageable level of pain to get through the day. I don't focus on the negative. I embrace the positive in EVERYTHING I DO. That attitude began when my lucidity returned in January 2004. I then realized that this was not some horrible nightmare I had just awaked from. It was the real deal and I was dying, like it or not. No one could believe I had lasted as long as I had.

102

I looked around that nursing home trapped in a wheel chair and realized this was all I had left and I was 52 years old. It was over. I had every good reason to just roll over and die. No one would have faulted me for that. I had a choice to make and it was a for real life or death choice. I CHOSE LIFE!

But then I was still faced with the reality that my body was irreparably damaged and was only getting worse. The stroke damage on top of the other problems made me the recipient of pity more than anything. I easily could have just accepted that and withered away until the lights went out for good. I figured I had nothing to lose by trying to do something, anything.

I literally had to start from the beginning like a newborn baby. I had to learn to read, write, do my numbers, button a button, zip a zipper, holding a pencil...EVERYTHING. Walking was

almost impossible. I say "almost"
because I did teach myself to hobble
around again.

The techniques I have outlined
above saved my life. If they can do
that you certainly can learn to throw
a baseball or hit a golf ball better.

We all paralyze ourselves
somewhat during our learning
process. Through trial and error we
learn to do things. Unfortunately, we
tend to store, too vividly, those
failures and when the crop up from
time to time they aren't just a film
clip, they are a full blown wide screen
70 mm movie! THAT is where the
problem lies...remembering our
failures. For some strange reasons
humans have been conditioned to
thrive on the negative side of life. We
rarely read about the wonderful
things that happen everyday. We
only hear about the tragedies. This
becomes our benchmark for how we
look at ourselves and the world
around us. I did it as well as anyone

until I was forced to change my thinking or die.

In improving your performance in anything you must focus on what works. If your focus is on telling yourself what TO DO and not what you shouldn't, your mindset is focused on a *positive* result rather than a negative. You should really eliminate the word "don't" from your performance vocabulary.

Imagine a golfer faced with a shot that has to get over water to be safe standing there telling himself, "Don't hit it in the water. Don't hit it in the water. Don't hit..." He has crippled himself with that sort of thinking.

He should have been saying, "That nice flat spot on the green." If he spent all of his thinking on actually rehearsing the trajectory of his shot soaring high and straight landing right where he intends it to, he would achieve that result more times than not. With the negative approach his chances at success go right down the drain.

106

THE WRAP UP

Since you have taken the time to get this far you obviously want to improve your performance. Using these techniques you can train yourself to get into the "zone" and perform at a level even you didn't think you could achieve. NO NEGATIVE THINKING ALLOWED!

Perseverance and practicing what works are the real keys to success. Winning thinking gives you a clear playing field upon which to build yourself into that kind of performer you really want to be. Understanding your limitations is a positive thing. Working to maximize your attributes is what you must strive for. Just as the 5' 4" basketball player has to use the playing strategy that suits his height limitation so should you work with what God gave you and use it to its maximum potential.

107

One thing is absolutely true, if you say you can or you say you can't, you're right. Giving up on anything is guaranteed failure. If you don't ask, you don't get. If you quit, it's over. Never give up! You have every good reason to succeed. You have just as much right to be the best you that you can possibly be. No one can stop you but you. Others may tell you that it is impossible and so what? Perhaps it is for them and if they have already thrown in the towel the match is over for them. Just because someone calls you an elephant you won't grow a trunk. No one has any power over your thinking but you. If you buy into the negativity that surrounds us all you will just become one more miserable face in the crowd.

You want to start right now in changing your attitude about life and yourself self image. You are a great and wonderful person. You have no good reason to be sour and angry. You have every good reason to be happy and proud of who you are and you abilities. Success comes to those who actively seek it. You can't even win the lottery if you don't buy a ticket. Everything requires ACTION.

I see so many people making all sorts of plans to do great things. Planning is all well and good. However, you don't make a career out of just making plans. You have to take action. You can walk all the way from Los Angeles to New York City one step at a time. The journey, as all journeys, starts with a singles step followed by another and still another until you reach your goal.

Setting goals for you is indeed important. But unless you actually start taking the steps to achieve your goal, you're standing still.

I find it very helpful each day when I wake up to think about how good it is just to be alive. Everything beyond that is a wonderful adventure. For the most part we all will eventually find what we are looking for and what I mean by saying that is, if you are looking for reasons why you can't do something or how it will never work you will indeed find them. The opposite is true as well. Winners think positively. They see life as a joy, a wonderment, and something to cherish.

Today is not a rehearsal for some grand day in the future. TODAY IS YOUR LIFE. Yesterday is a memory and tomorrow may not be there so it is incumbent upon us all to live each day to its fullest. I hate having to go to sleep! I am as I was as a little boy...thrilled with what lies ahead for me each day! I welcome everything. The joy and sadness life brings are things to cherish. Knowing the techniques to interact with others in a helpful and compassionate way make you a person others seek out and want to be around. Being a pleasant successful person should be everyone's ultimate goal each and

every day. We can't have too of those
people. You can be one of them
starting right now.

I overcame cancer and a stroke.
I play and teach golf. I write books. I
visit schools and talk to little kids. I
volunteer at nursing homes. I LIVE.
When there is a bump in the road I
know what to do to not make myself
crazy over it. I use these techniques
all day everyday and so should you.
It is a great feeling to walk into a
room and see happy faces.

I have a "daily" that I do and
you should consider it as part of your
own daily routine. Everyday I make it
a point to compliment two strangers.
It is always something simple, honest
and quick. Standing in line at the
store I may see a lady with a pretty
sweater and all I say to her is, "That
sweater really looks nice on you."
And then I smile and turn away. That
person's day will be a tiny bit
brighter. She knows I was honest and
wasn't "hitting on her". Sincere

compliments help YOU. You are adding to the positive in the world in a small way. It is infectious. You don't have to go out of your way to do this or keep a scorecard. You just do it when it feels right. I just want to plant the seed for you here as I am sure once you add this little thing to your daily routine you'll feel better about yourself and that is what this whole book is about.

I would think that the most important thing anyone can do to begin to achieve happiness and success is to sit down, take a pencil and paper and contemplate what it is that you find bring you the most happiness. Be honest with yourself about those activities that you do that are the most enjoyable. The best part of this is that there are no wrong answers. The list doesn't need to be long but it must be those things that are indeed the most important to you.

Examples would be golfing, running, fishing, sewing, cooking, reading...whatever you find to be the most enjoyable.

The reason you want this list is so you can always refer to it when you are in need of doing something good for you. When I find myself in situations where I am not obtaining any positive benefit I refer to my list and choose something there as a substitute. I may not be able to get to it right away but I make it a point not to cheat myself out of enjoying life.

Too many of us are so wrapped up in collecting stuff. When I lay dying most of my stuff was given away or sold off since I wouldn't need it anymore. If you spend your life in the constant pursuit of collecting stuff (houses, portfolios, cars, whatever) you are missing what I call the "JUICE OF LIFE". We all strive to be comfortable and have nice things. But to substitute your life in exchange for building a collection only causes you to forfeit another moment you could have been enjoying yourself doing something on your list.

If you are so caught up in status and keeping up with the Joneses you're self esteem has a lot of work that needs work. When you put "stuff" into its proper perspective ask yourself, "When was the last time you were impressed seeing some stranger sitting behind to wheel of a new Rolls Royce waiting for a red light?" More than likely you weren't. If fact, you probably drew a conclusion that the person behind the wheel had serious self esteem issues. To take this a step down, remember that one man's Ford is another man's Rolls. So never discount the fact that your "status" is envied by someone else no matter how low you may thing you are on the ladder of life.

114

If you concentrate on being the kindest, happiest person you can be I am sure you will find that reward enough for your time here. Remember, there are no scorecards at any cemetery. Your happiness is with you, always inside of you. Your most important contribution to the world is being the kindest, happiest you that you can be. There is no substitute.

If you are centered emotionally and happy, armed with the interpersonal techniques and skills to work through even the most trying interpersonal confrontations, what could be nicer? A happy person is a confident person and a person who is confident has the best chance at performing consistently at his highest level.

115

So your first task is to get happy. From there everything else can flow. Understanding your state is a choice now gives you the power to choose whichever state you like. To begin making your list I would strongly recommend that you do this when you are in a happy state. If you are in a good mood to begin with it will make it easier for you to focus on all of those things that bring you happiness. Also make this list while you are alone. You don't need anyone standing over your shoulder commenting on what your preferences are. Nor do you want their input. This is YOUR LIST.

You may want to have an opening sentence like, "I am most happy when I am..." and fill in the blank.

This is your private list and you would be best advised to keep it to yourself and also handy for those rare moments when you are feeling the need for something happier.

Michael Cortson

116

Many of the techniques discussed here are used in Neuro Linguistic Programming, or NLP for short. There are many NLP coaches who specialize in helping people just like you who are serious about taking charge of the life.

Always remember you are so unique there is only one of you therefore you are special. No one else does it to you. We are all 100% responsible for ourselves. You have every good reason to be happy. You have the tools to communicate emotions and listen to emotions. You are a kind person and you want to spread kindness wherever you go. You are persistent, directed and will never give up. You are a winner!

[*1] *Eye and Head Turning Indicates Cerebral Lateralization*; Kinsbourne, M., **Science**, 179, pp. 539541, 1972.
Lateral Eye Movement and Cognitive Mode; Kocel, K., et al., **Psychon Sci.** 27: pp. 223224, 1972.
Individual Differences in Cognitive Style_Reflective Eye Movements; Galin, D. and Ornstein, R., **Neuropsychologia**, 12, pp. 376397, 1974.
The Effect of Eye Placement On Orthographic Memorization; Loiselle, François, Ph.D. Thesis, Faculté des Sciences Sociales, Université de Moncton, New Brunswick, Canada, 1985.
Eye Movement As An Indicator of Sensory Components in Thought; Buckner, W., Reese, E. and Reese, R., **Journal of Counseling Psychology**, 1987, Vol. 34, No 3.